The Visions Coloring Book
By Stephen Beam

The Visions Coloring Book

By Stephen Beam

Copyright © 2016

2 Corinthians 12 (NIV)
2)I know a man in Christ who fourteen years ago was caught up to the third heaven. Whether it was in the body or out of the body I do not know—God knows. 3)And I know that this man—whether in the body or apart from the body I do not know, but God knows— 4)was caught up to paradise and heard inexpressible things, things that no one is permitted to tell.

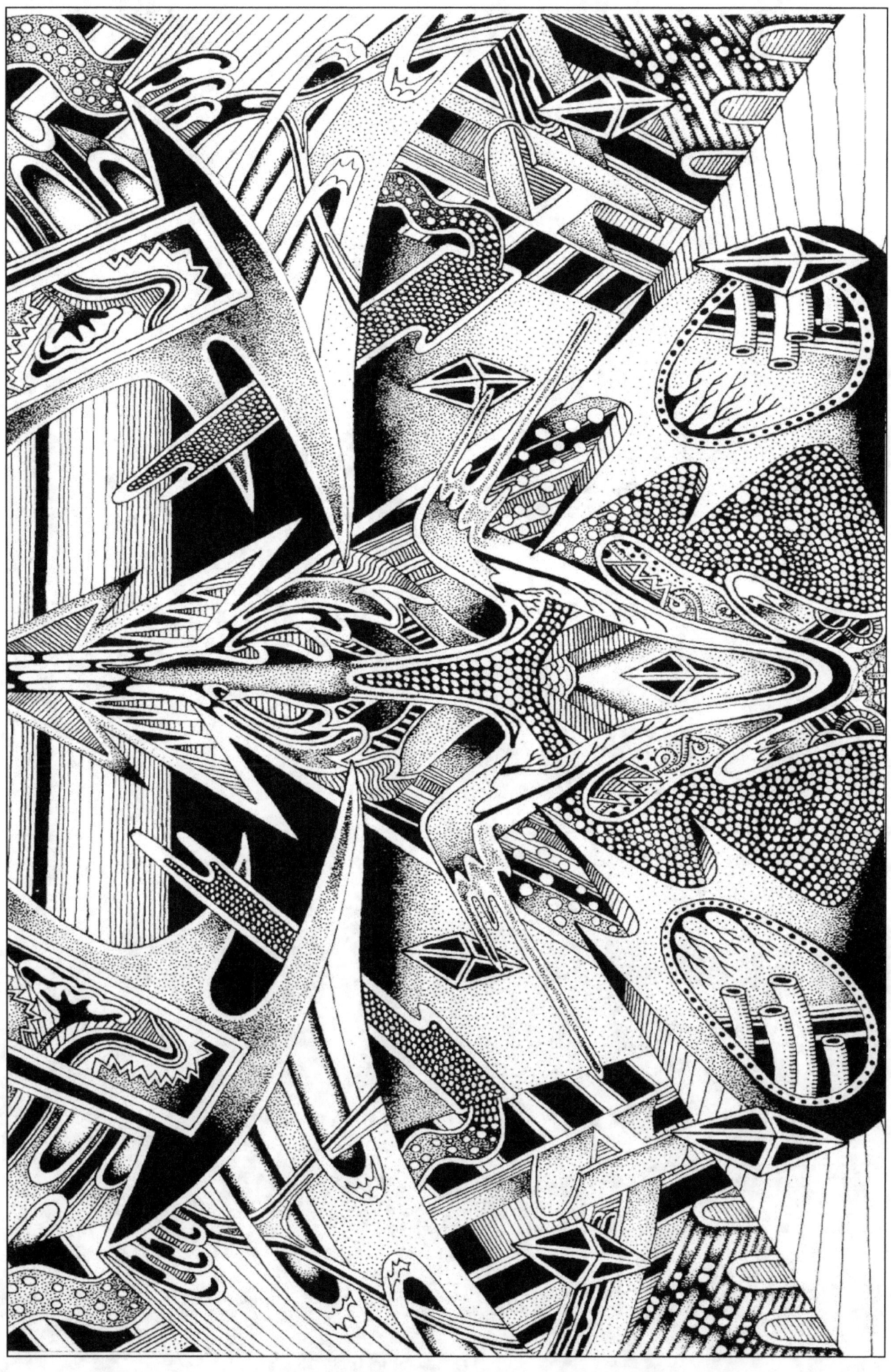

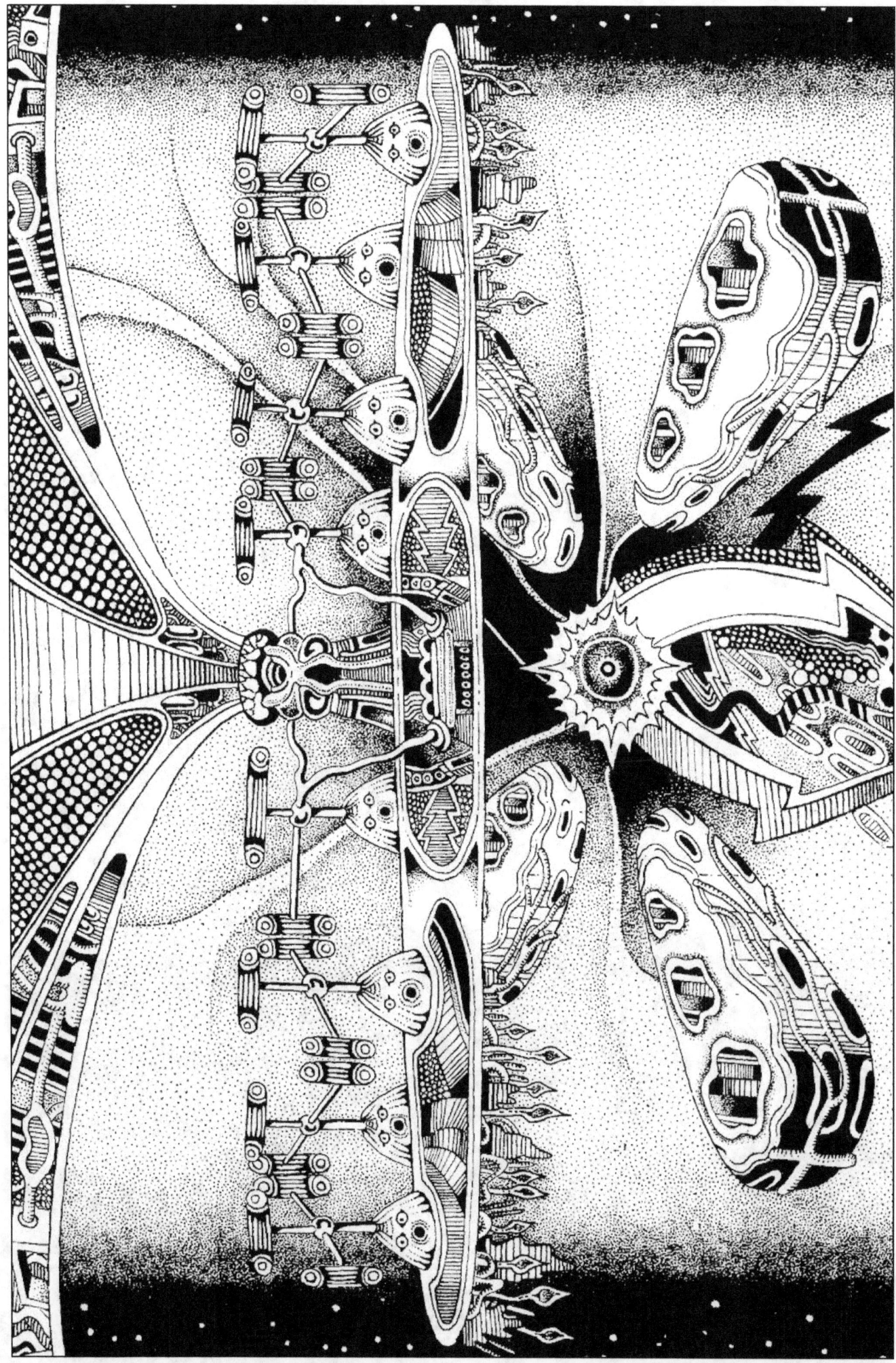

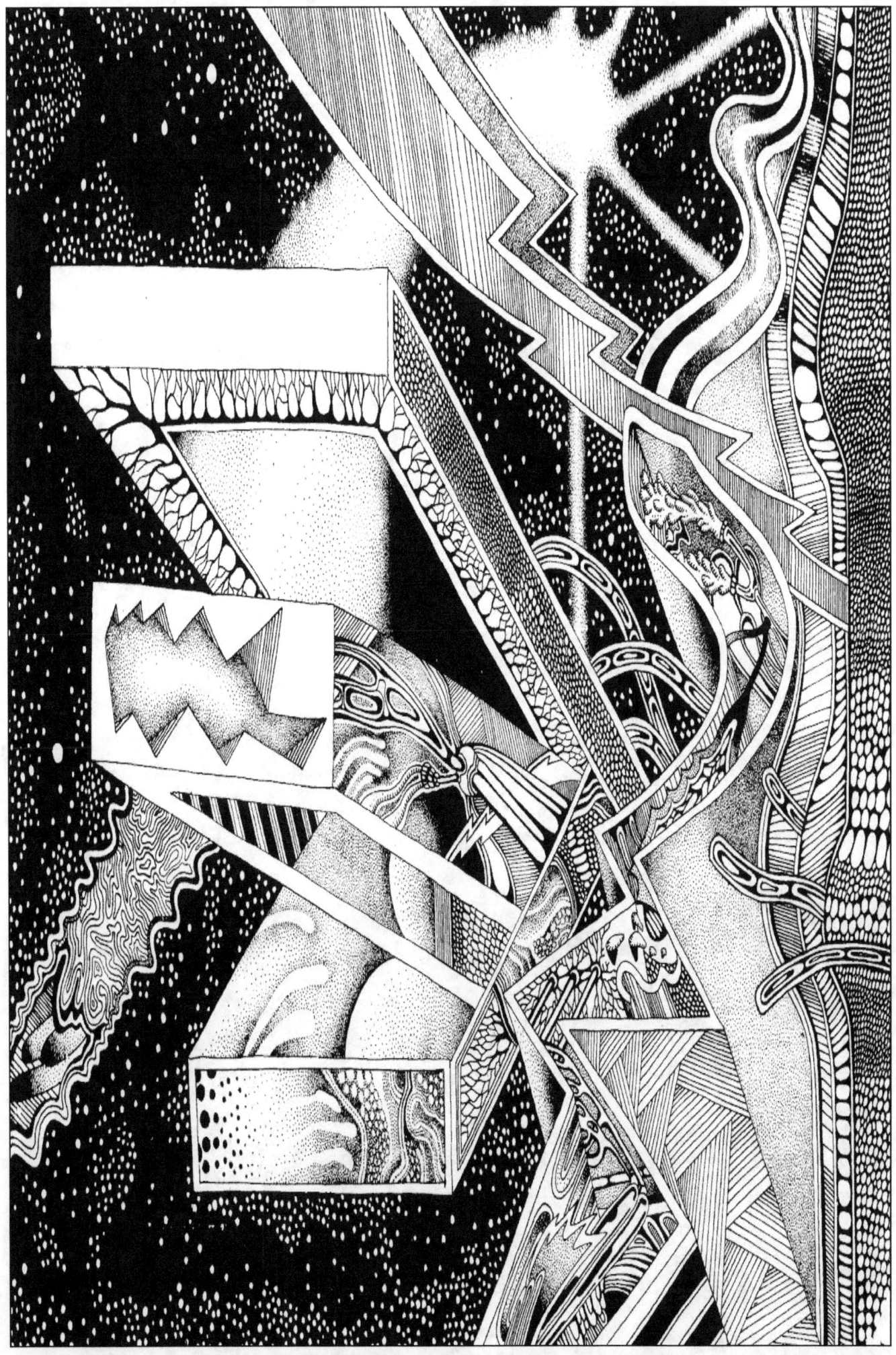

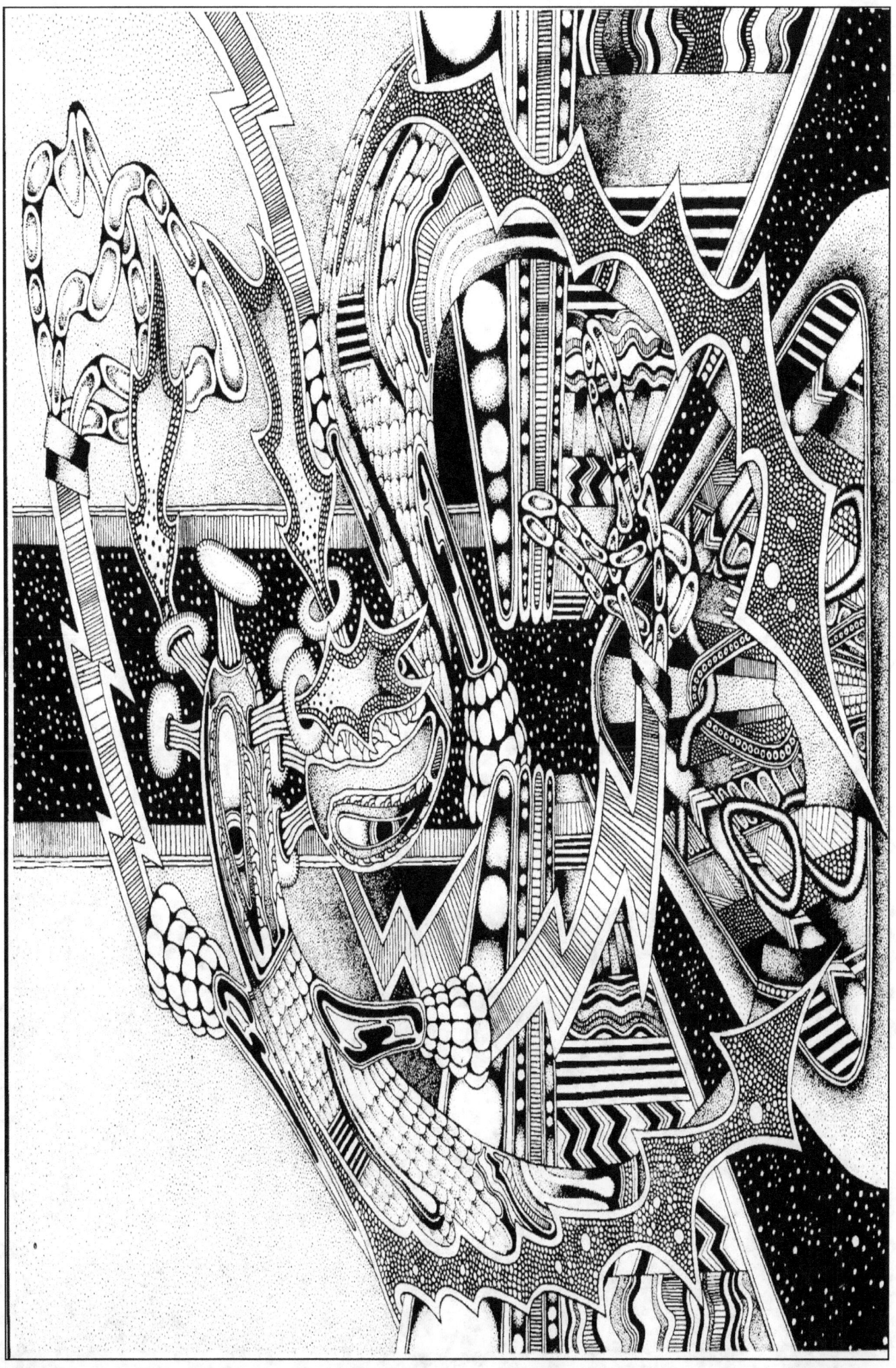

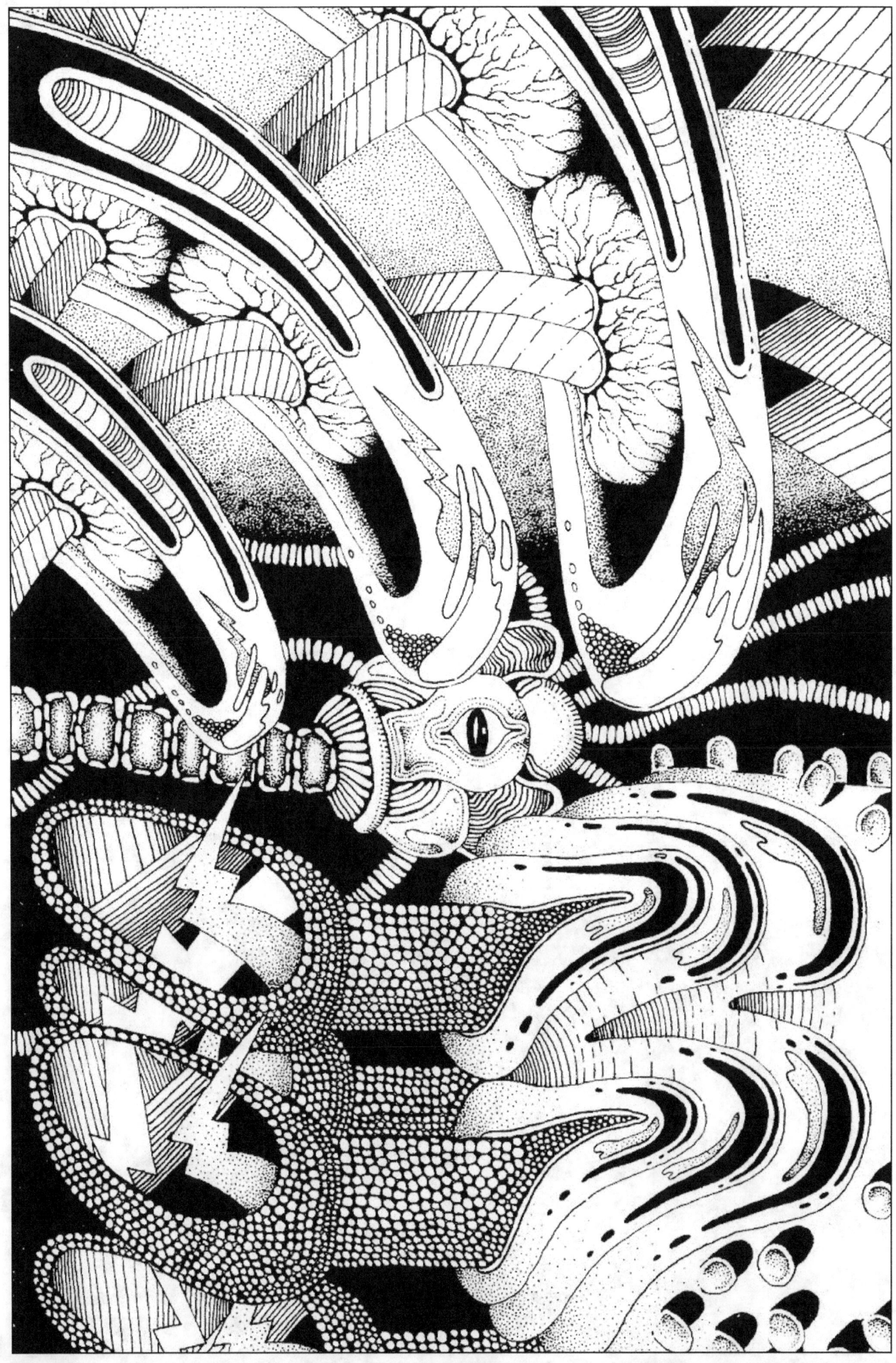

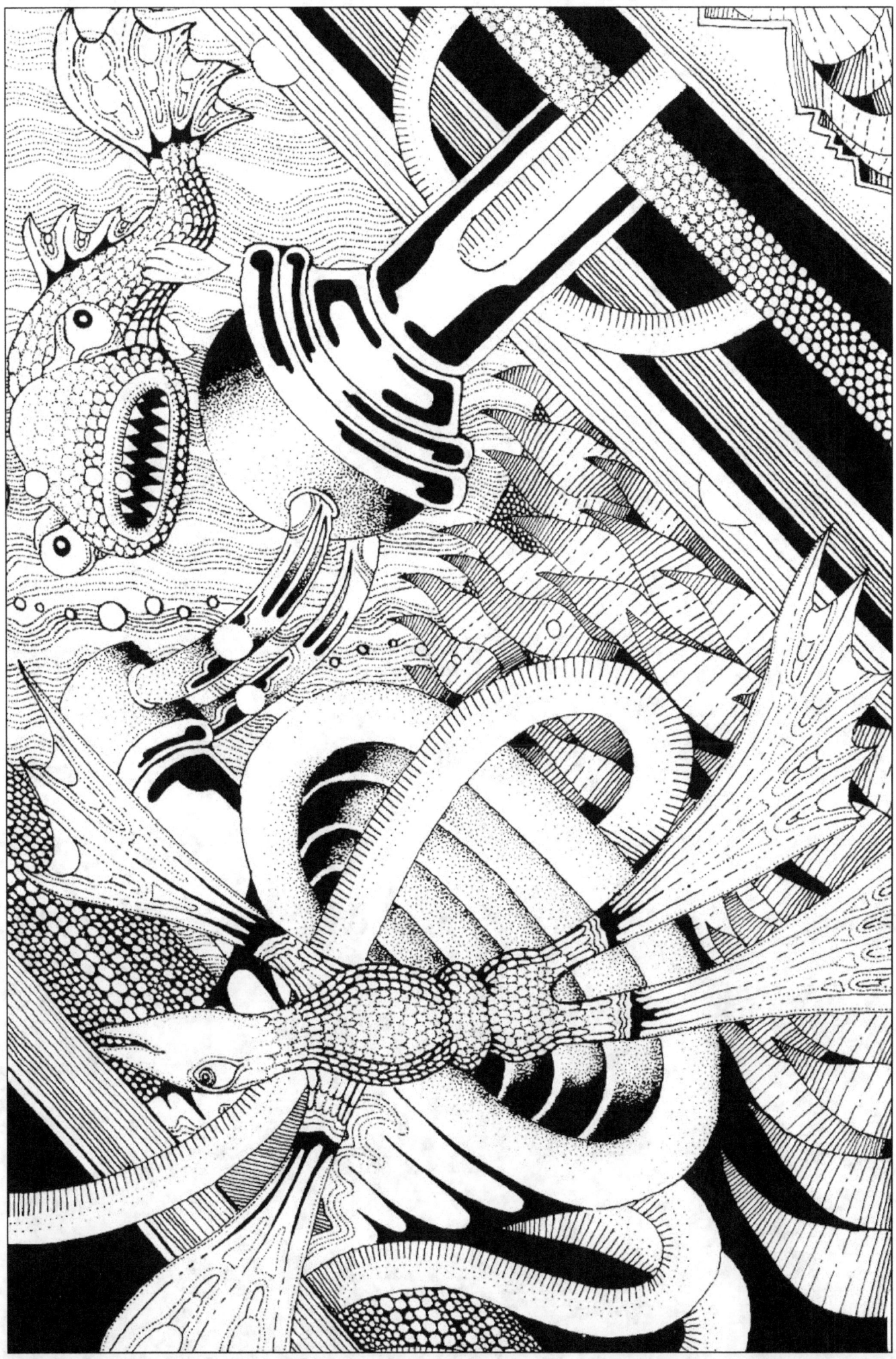

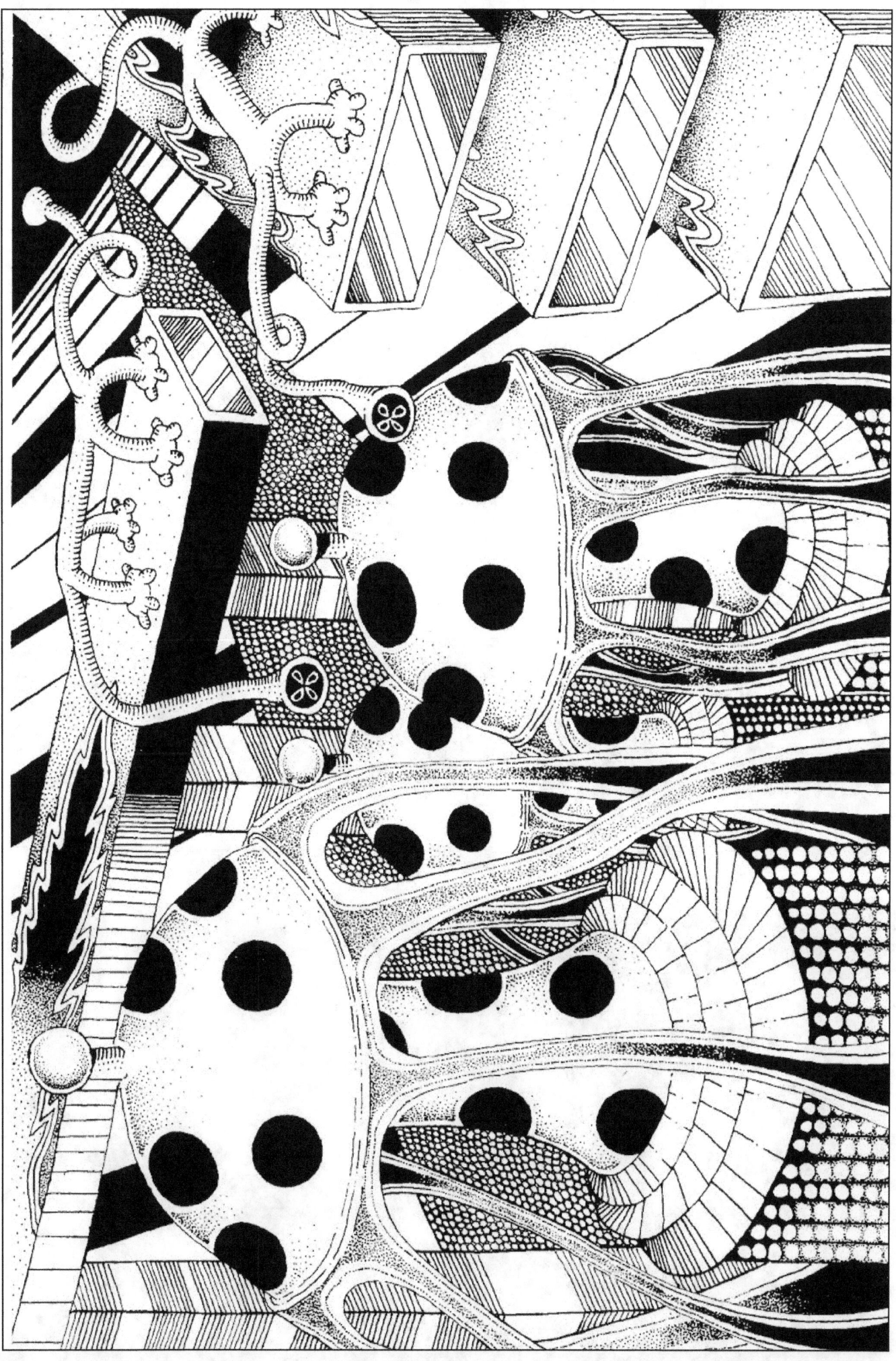

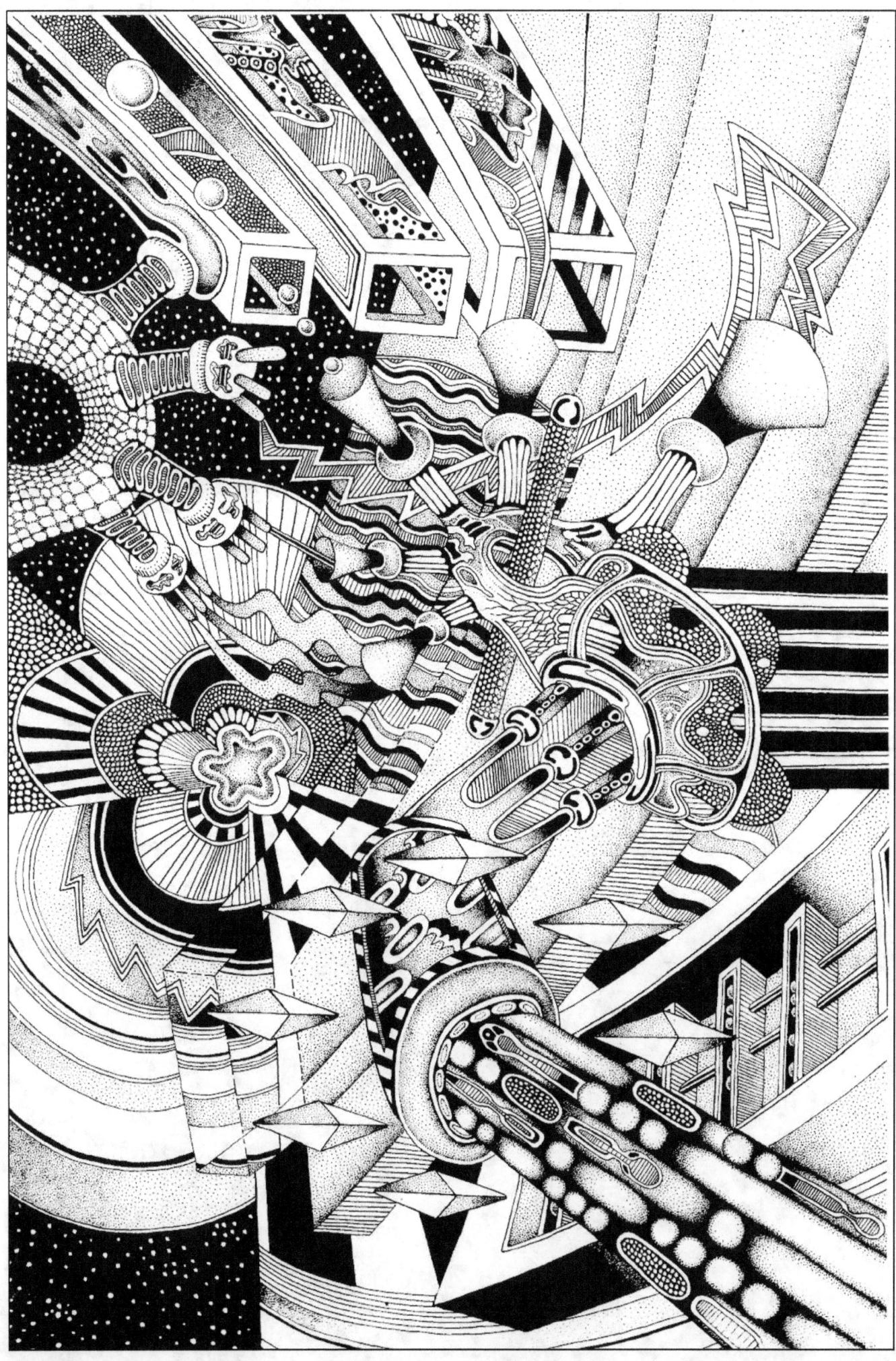

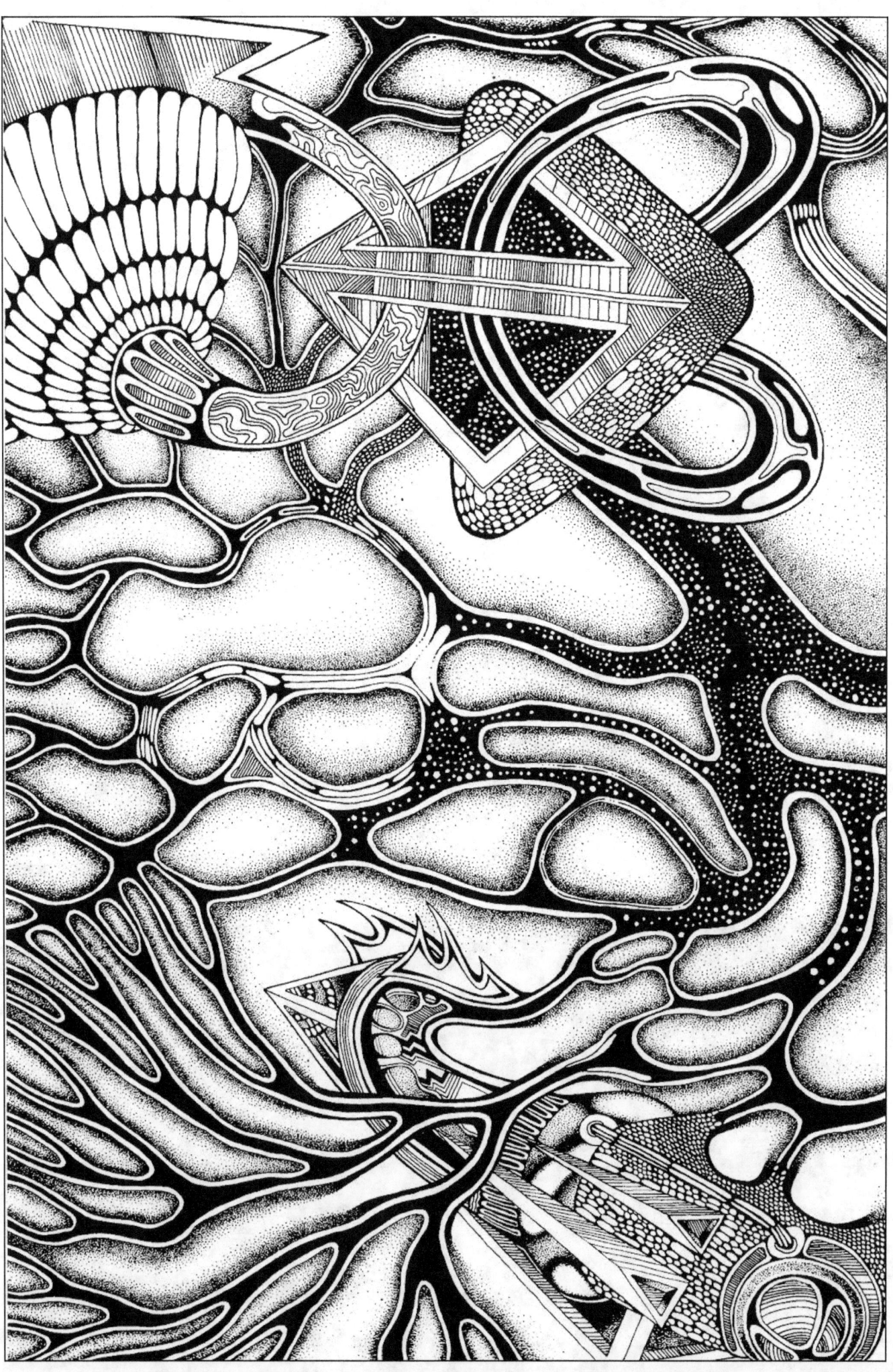

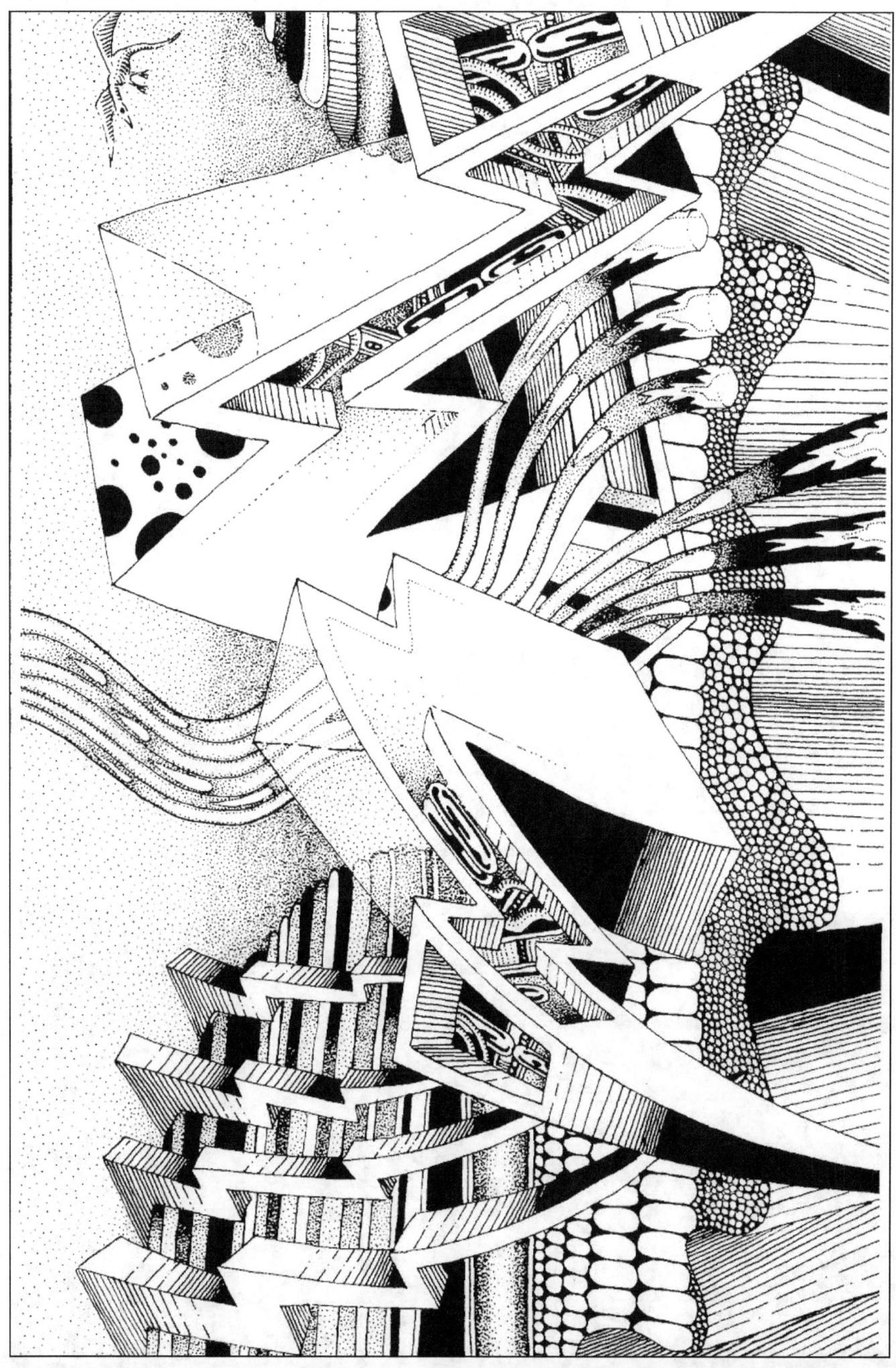

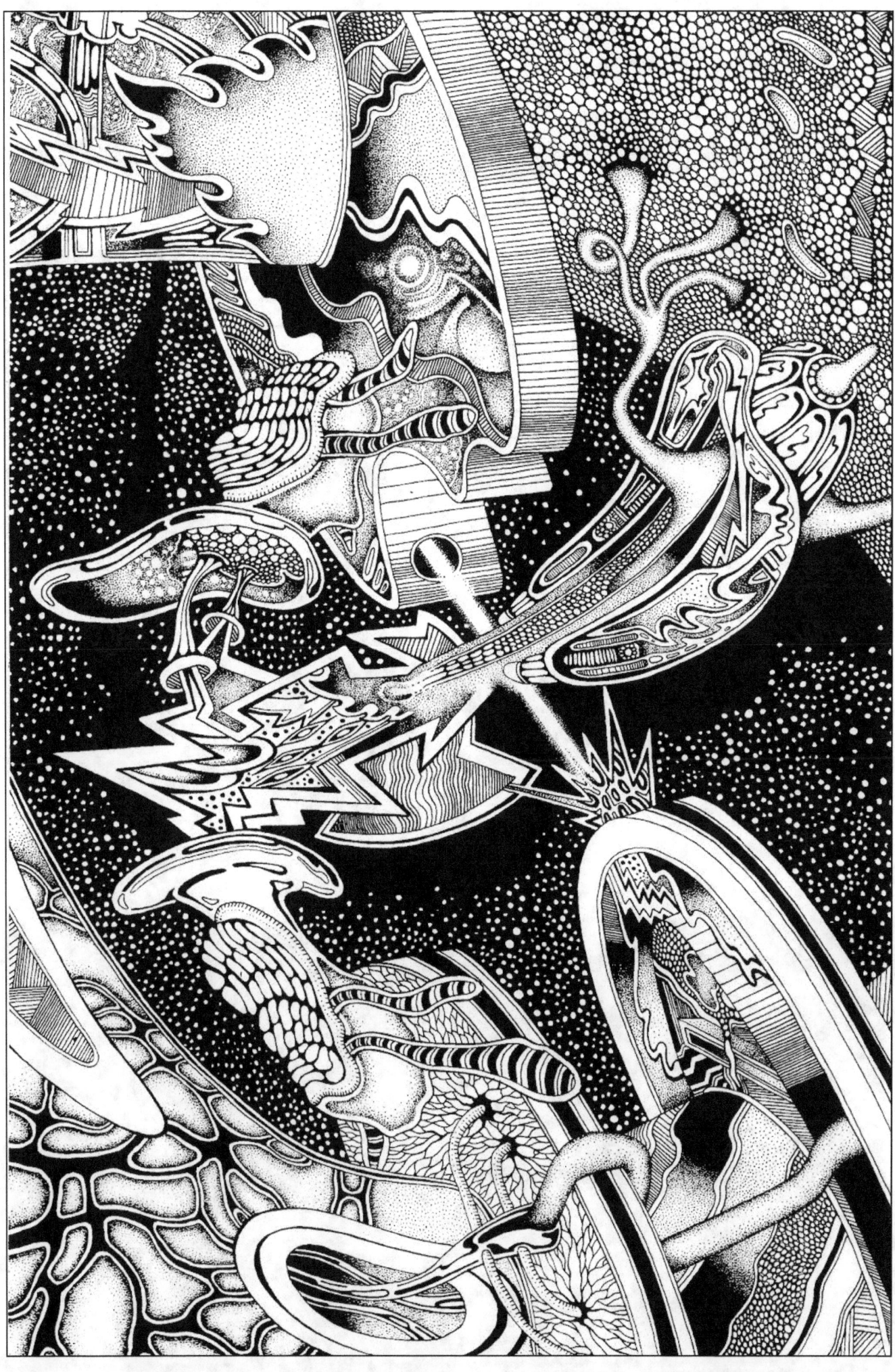

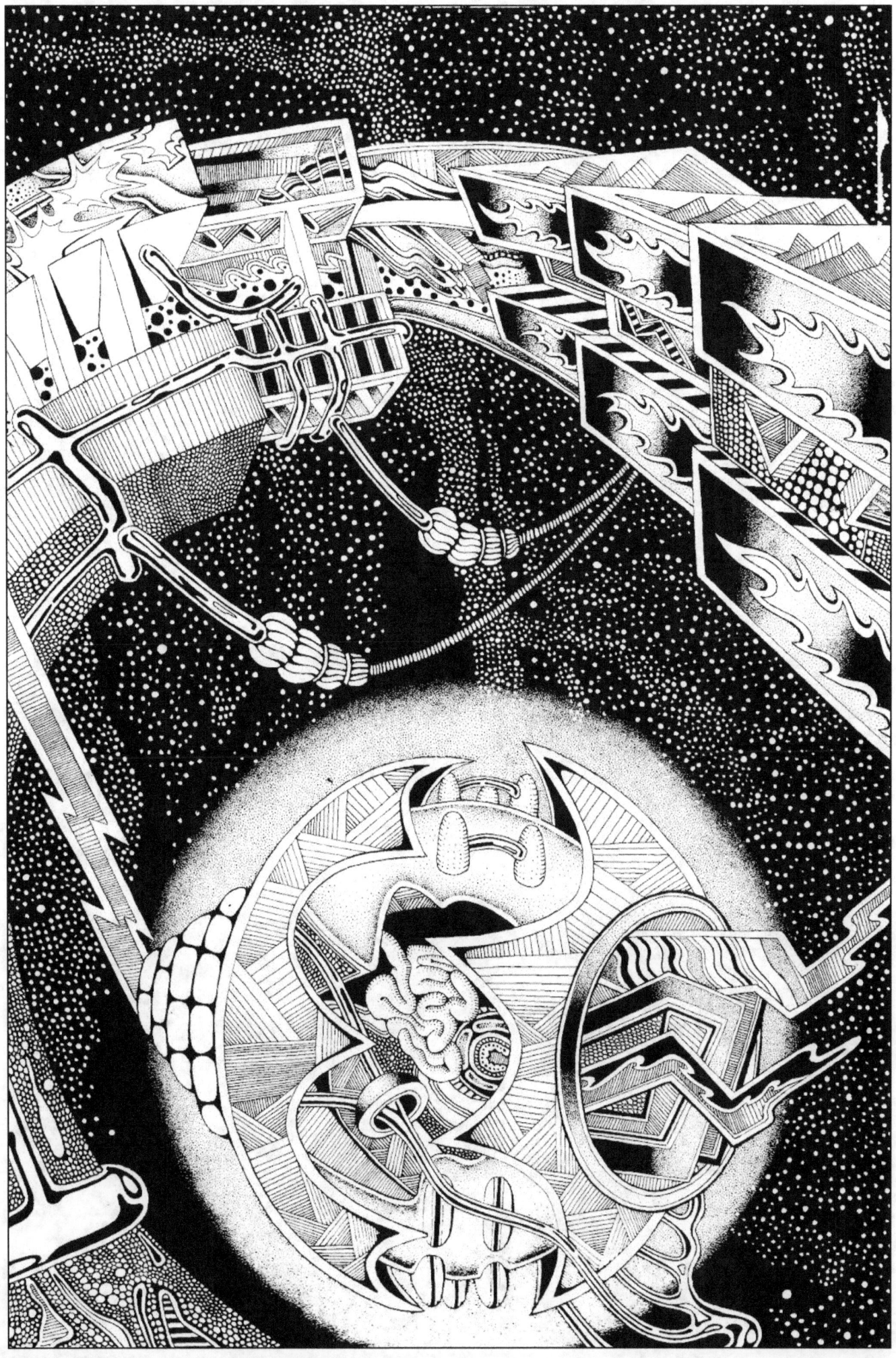

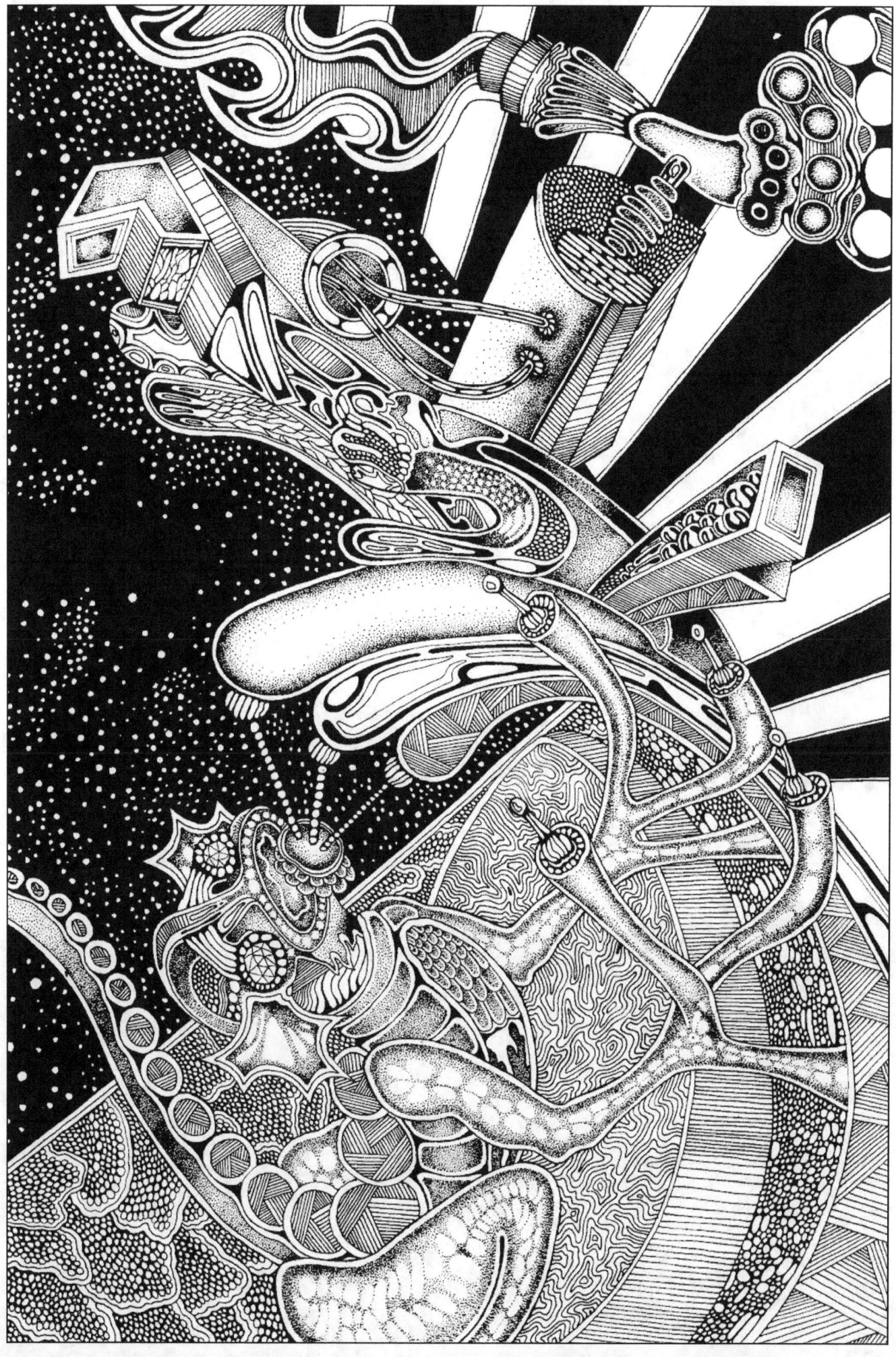

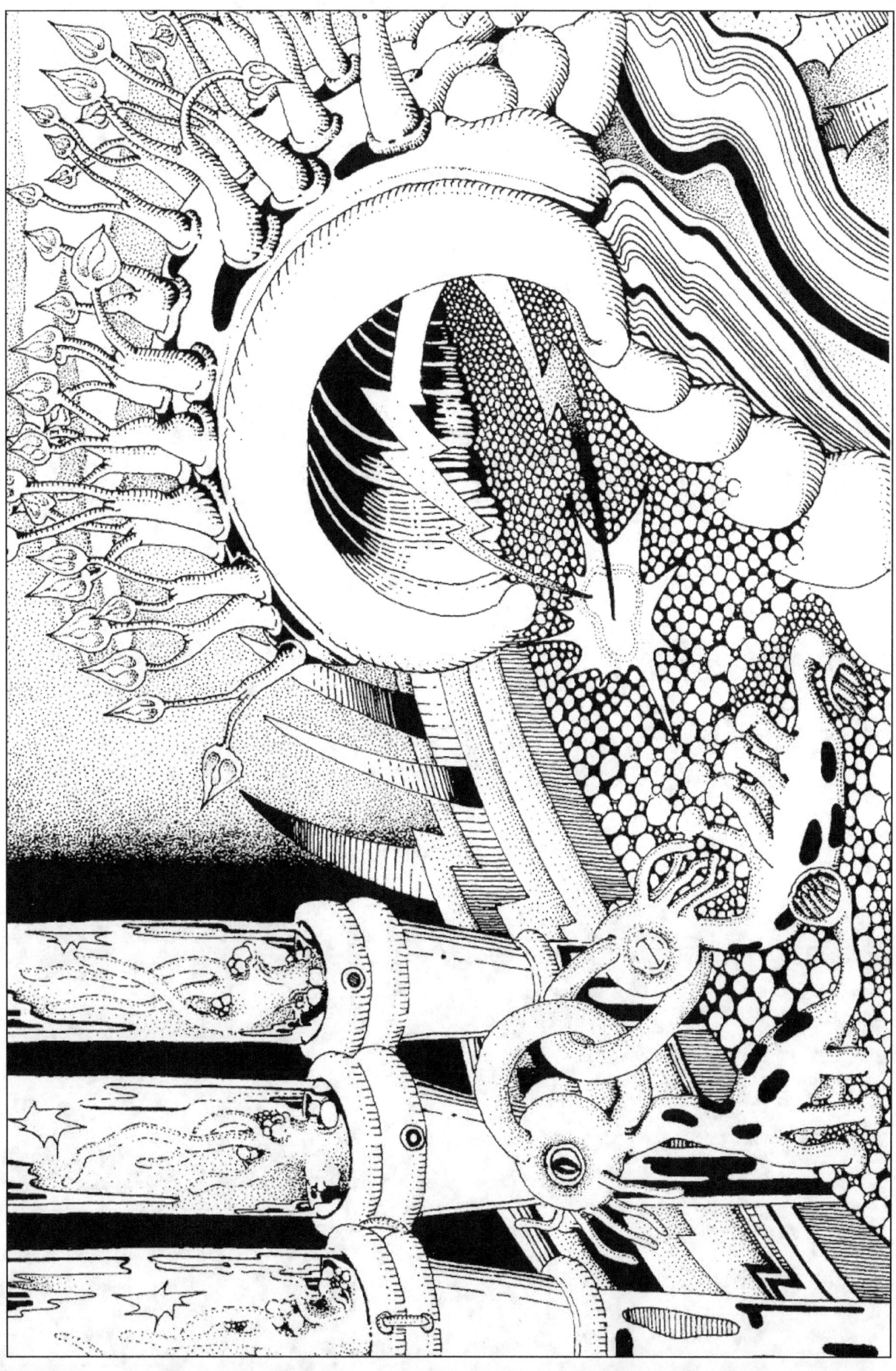

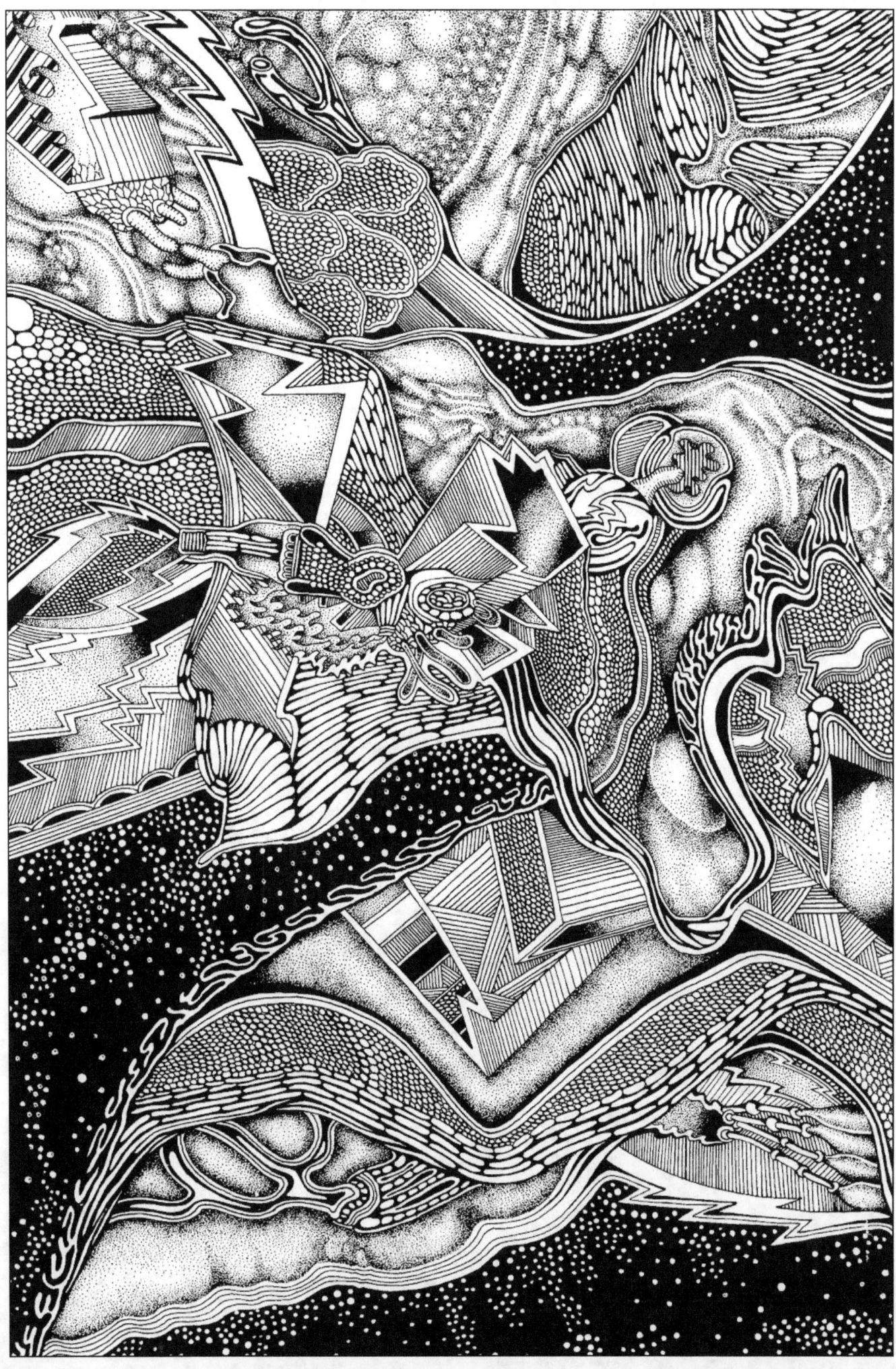

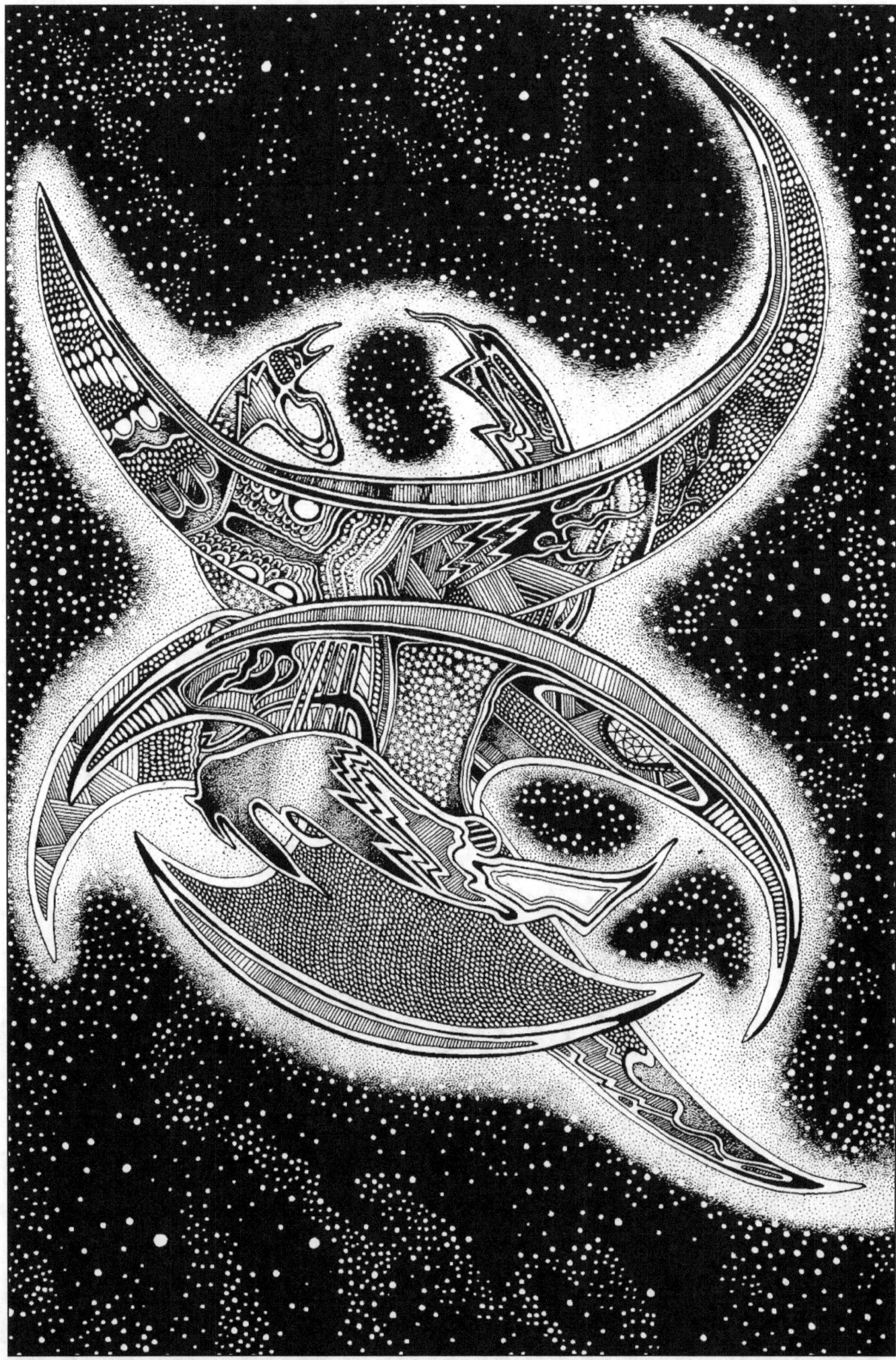

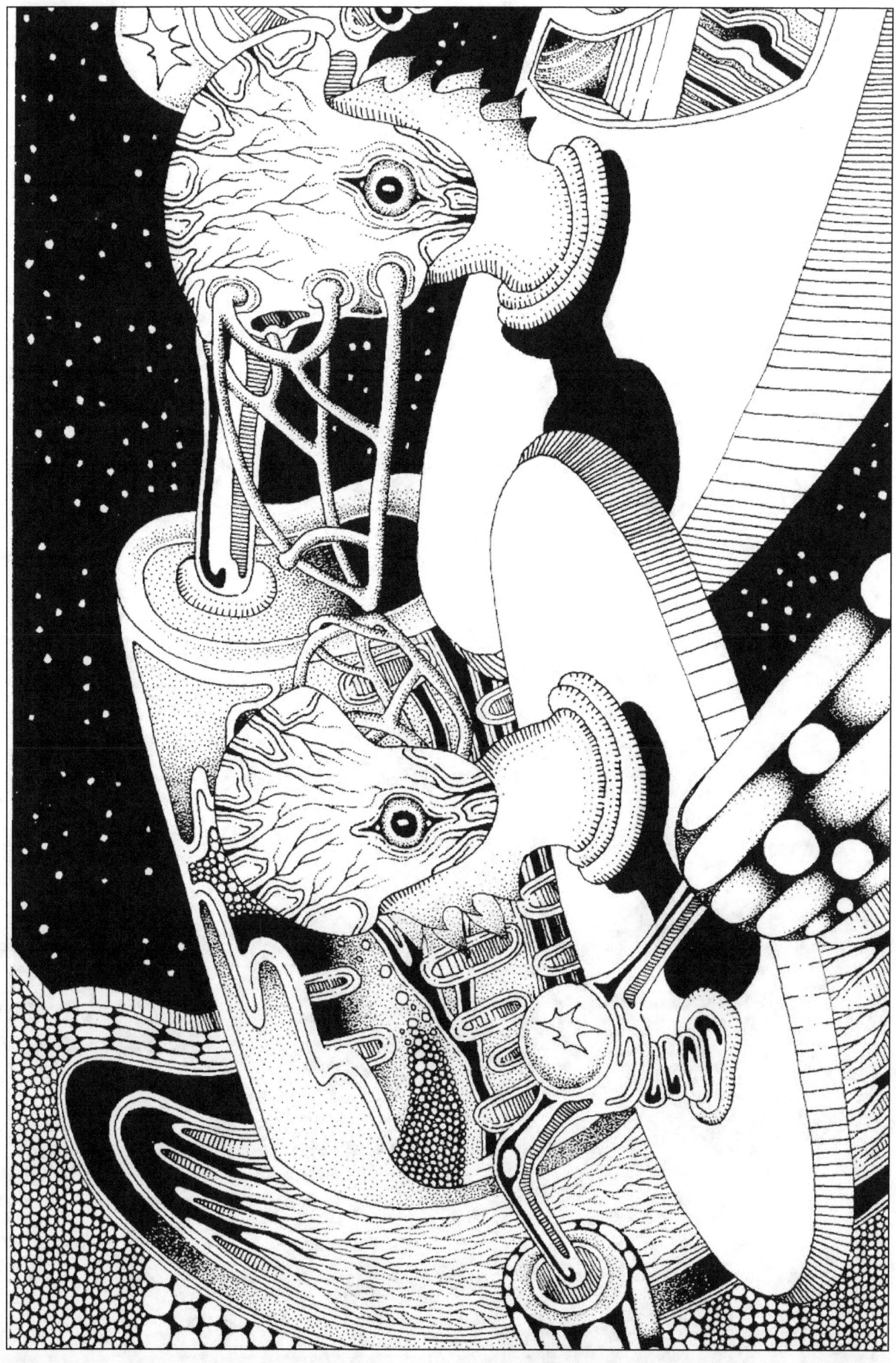

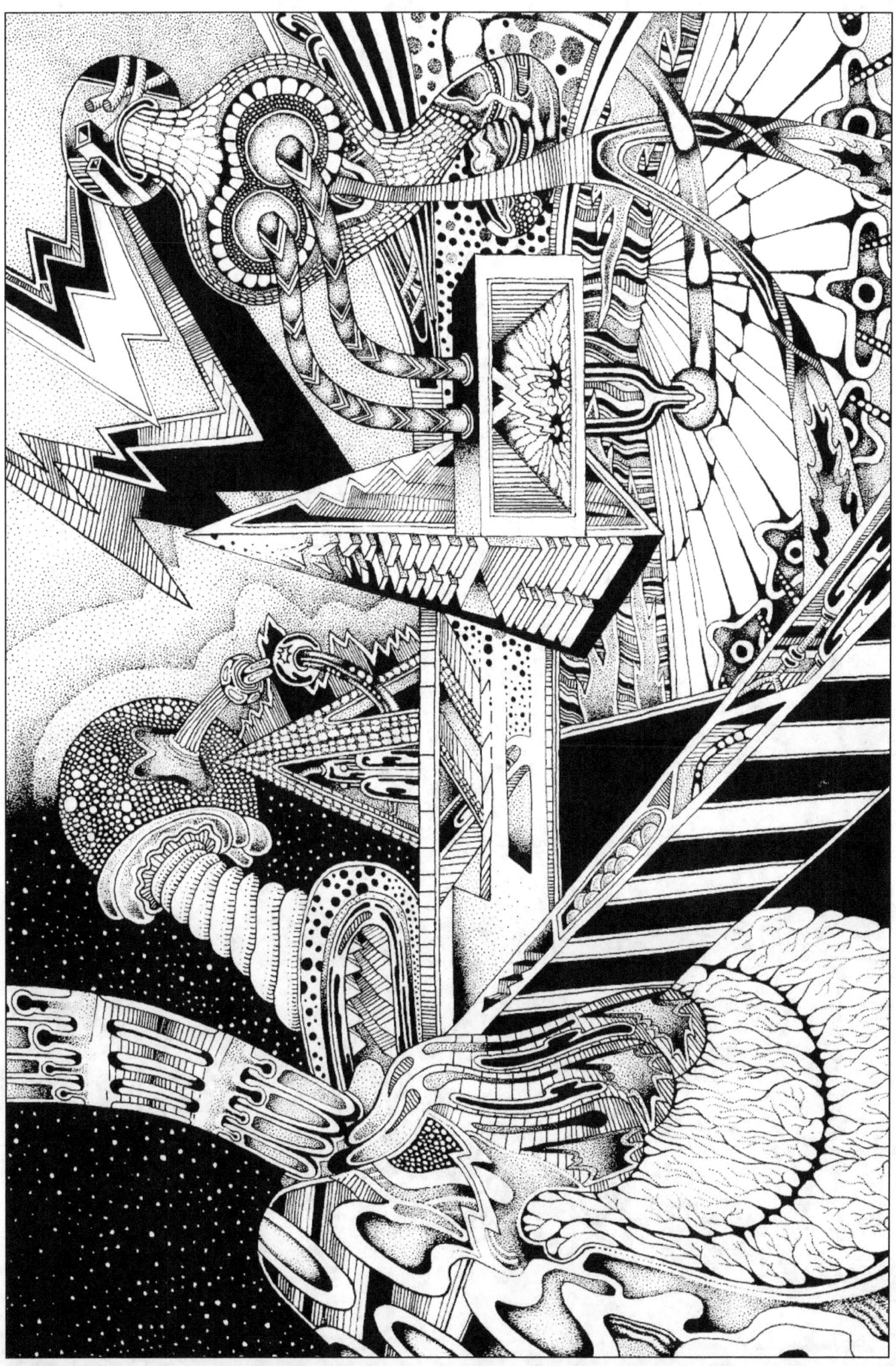

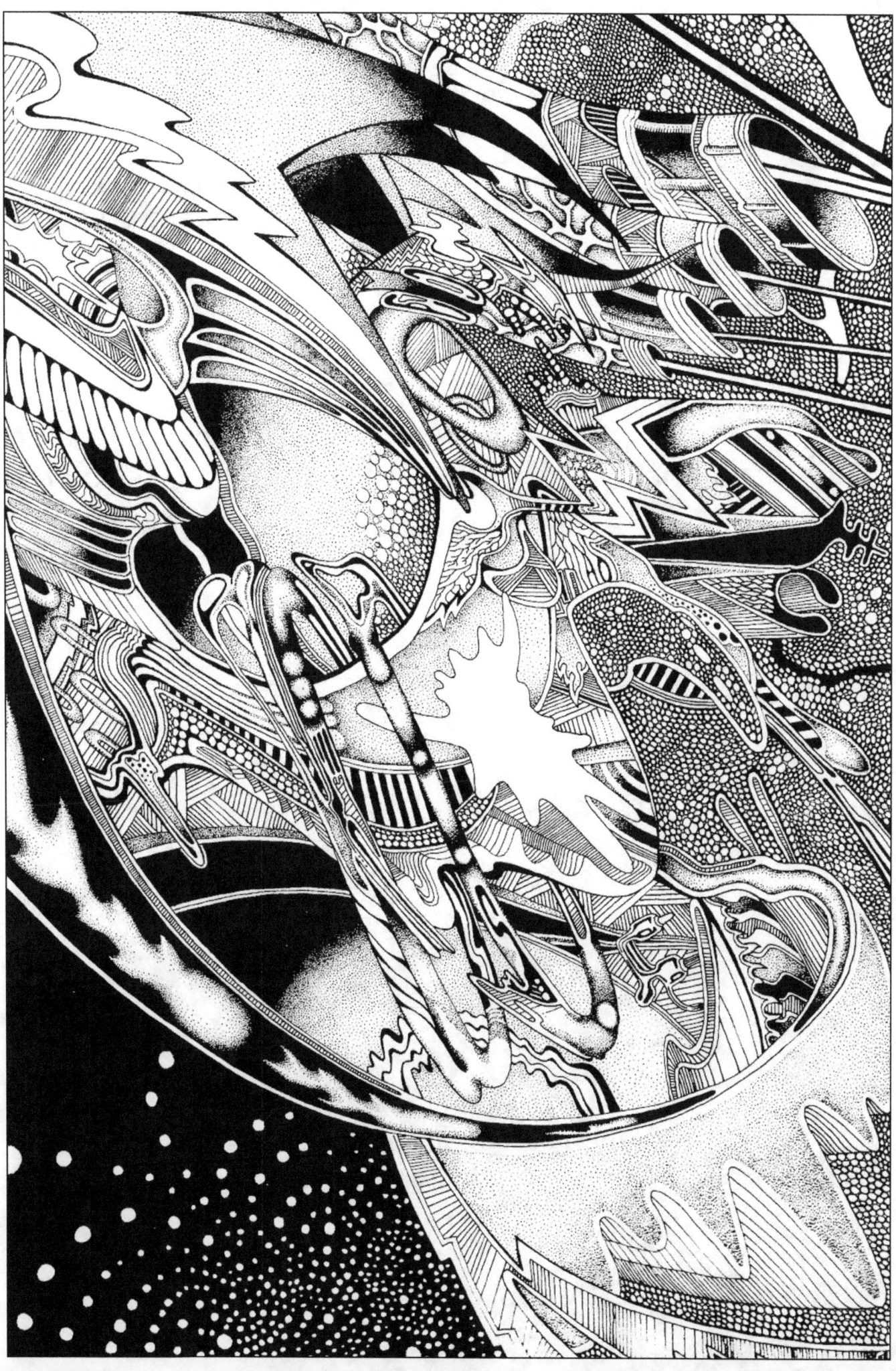

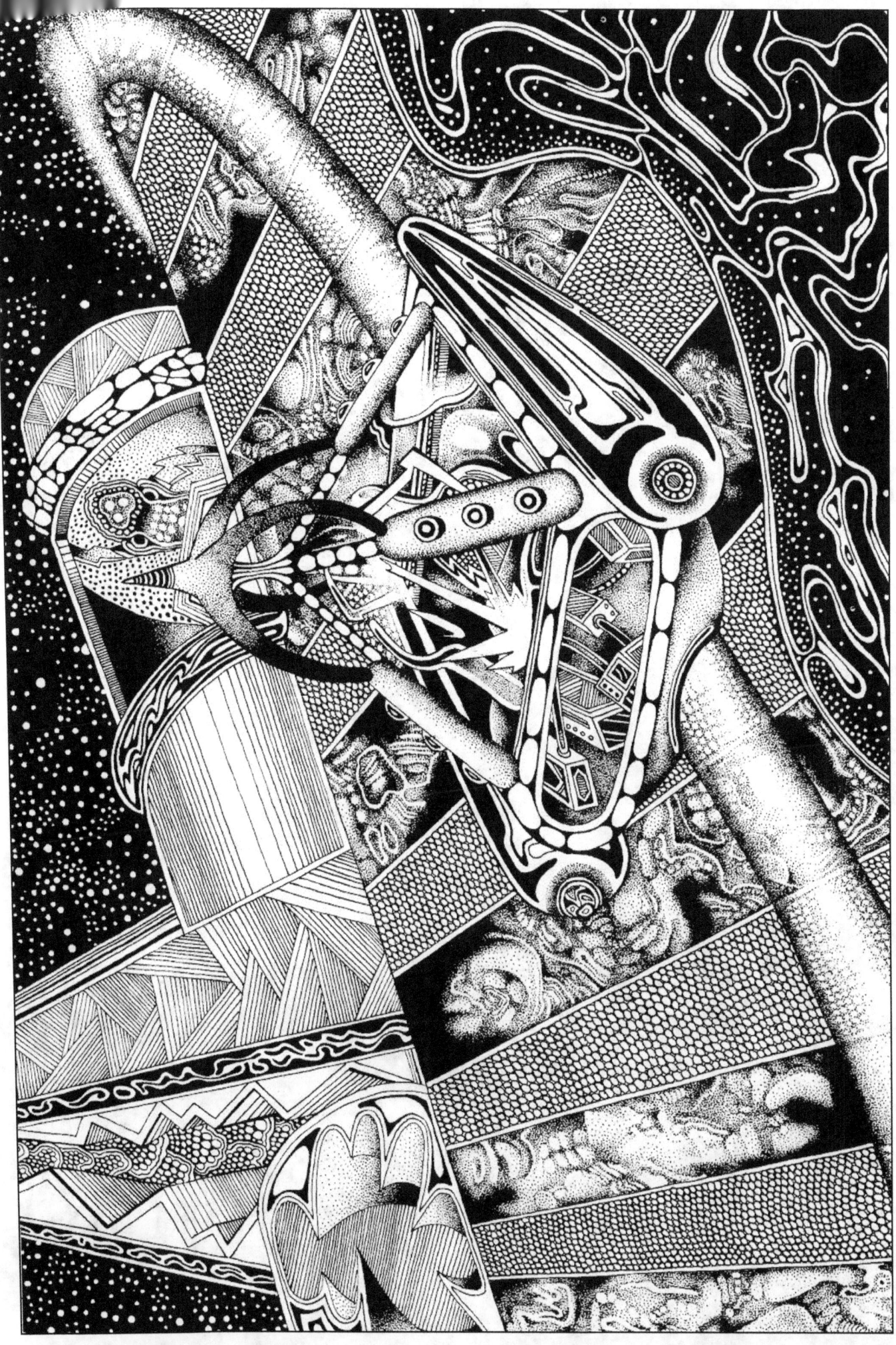

Ezekiel 1 (NIV)

17) As they moved, they would go in any one of the four directions the creatures faced; the wheels did not change direction as the creatures went. 18) Their rims were high and awesome, and all four rims were full of eyes all around. 19) When the living creatures moved, the wheels beside them moved; and when the living creatures rose from the ground, the wheels also rose.

~ Sweet Dreams ~